TREETOPS

Time Chronicles

The Cauldron of Darkness

Written by Roderick Hunt
and illustrated by Alex Brychta

OXFORD
UNIVERSITY PRESS

OXFORD
UNIVERSITY PRESS

Great Clarendon Street, Oxford OX2 6DP, United Kingdom

Oxford University Press is a department of the University of Oxford. It furthers the University's objective of excellence in research, scholarship, and education by publishing worldwide. Oxford is a registered trade mark of Oxford University Press in the UK and in certain other countries

First Edition published in 2012

British Library Cataloguing in Publication Data

Data available

ISBN: 978-0-19-8475729

10 9 8 7 6 5 4 3 2 1

Printed in China by Imago

Paper used in the production of this book is a natural, recyclable product made from wood grown in sustainable forests. The manufacturing process conforms to the environmental regulations of the country of origin.

Acknowledgements: The publisher and authors would like to thank the following for their permission to reproduce photographs and other copyright material:

P46 Mary Evans Picture Library/Alamy; TsR/Shutterstock; Valentin Agapov/Shutterstock; magicinfoto/Shutterstock; Picsfive/Shutterstock; North Wind Picture Archives/Alamy; Art Directors & TRIP/Alamy; Heritage Images/Corbis; David Prince/Corbis; **PP46-47** Jakub Krechowicz/Shutterstock; Blaz Kure/Shutterstock; **P47** Ragnarock/Shutterstock; Mary Evans Picture Library

Chapter 1

Then the Darkness spoke.

The Darkness was everywhere, but it was nowhere. It had no voice, yet its thoughts were at one with every Viran. The thoughts that entered each Viran's dark mind were these: "We have been thwarted in our purpose because of children. Our quests have failed despite our careful planning, despite long preparation.

"We have not been vigilant enough. We thought the Time Guardians were defeated. We did not allow for Mortlock's cunning."

As the Darkness hissed the name 'Mortlock', it was as if an electric shock passed through each Viran everywhere. Inside the vat in the Time Vault laboratory, forks of black lighting crackled and spat, making the vat shake and tremble.

"Mortlock has regained his strength! Children have become his warriors. He has trained the children to capture us."

Each Viran's thoughts were the same at that moment. "But how could *children* ...?"

"A device called a Zaptrap. It looks like a steel ball. The children throw it. It opens and emits a pulse. This destabilizes us and returns us to raw matter.

"But Mortlock has made a fatal error," hissed the Darkness. "The energy that has been captured in his glass vat has fused together. It is now able to communicate. Each Viran captured by the children adds to our knowledge of them, so we learn more about who they are."

The Virans' thoughts merged together as one: "These children must be eliminated."

The Darkness hissed, "They must! But we are Virans. Attack them directly and our Viran natures would be revealed. No! The children must be destroyed the Viran way."

Chapter 2

Wilma was woken from a dream by the alarm sounding in her sleep pod. Sleepily she hit the cancel button and turned over, pulling her duvet over her head.

Then a second alarm went off. Wilma sat bolt upright in bed. It was a red alert. The LED on the wall was flashing: "Urgent! Report at once to Room X."

Wilma sprang out of bed and dressed as quickly as she could. An alarm call from Mortlock, especially so early in the day, meant something serious had happened.

With her trainer laces still untied, she slide down the chute that connected the sleep pods to the Control Room. Tyler was not there, nor were any of the others. They must be in Room X already.

Wilma ran through the Library and raced along the corridor. Behind her came the sound of running feet. It was Chip. He was stuffing his T-shirt into his jeans as he ran.

"It must be serious," panted Chip. "'Cos Mortlock's never called a red before."

"And why in Room X of all places?" gasped Wilma as she pulled open the heavy doors to the room.

Room X was where objects from magic key adventures were on display. The children rarely, if ever, went inside it.

The others were there already. Tyler shot a warning glance towards Mortlock, who was standing perfectly still with his eyes closed. He was holding Wilf's skateboard. Floppy sat at his feet. Then Mortlock took off his glasses and spoke.

"I could not have asked for braver or more loyal children than you have proved to be," he said. "You have been resourceful and resilient. Your courage has never faltered. But now, I cannot expect you to continue. It is wrong of me to put you in so much danger. Because of my stupidity, the Virans know it is you who are capturing them."

"But how can that be?" asked Neena.

"The dark matter in the vat has been behaving oddly – fizzing, boiling like a strange cauldron of darkness," said Mortlock. "It may have become a source of Viran intelligence. I cannot be sure, but I think it may be able to communicate."

"So it sends messages to other Virans?" suggested Nadim. "Like telepathy?"

"I couldn't have put it better, Nadim," said Mortlock. "It's bad news. If the Viran memories in the vat are fused together, and can communicate, then all Virans will know exactly who you are."

Wilf had an idea. "Hang on! Whenever we go back in history, we change. OK, we stay the same inside, but we just look like any other kid at that time."

"Wilf is right," said Biff. "If the Virans become wary of children, it'll be easier for us to spot them. They may act suspiciously whenever children are around."

"So we're staying on as Time Runners," said Wilma. "We'll just have to be extra careful on the missions."

Mortlock looked thoughtful. "Are you sure? Because if you want to leave the Time Vault now, then I will understand."

"We're staying," said Kipper. "Who else have you got to fight the Virans?"

"Thank 'eavens!" said Tyler. "Who would I argue with if you lot went?"

Chapter 3

For a while, things were quiet. From time to time the children would pop into Control to chat with Tyler, who spent most of his time keeping a watchful eye on the beautiful hologram thrown up by the TimeWeb.

"'Cos no one else can read it like I can," he would say. And he was right, for something that no one else would have noticed suddenly caught his eye. He pressed the alarm.

"It's something new," said Tyler when the others had gathered round the TimeWeb. "It's not really a spot, more a very fine grey circle. It's so small, you can hardly see it."

"I can't make it out," said Biff. "Where is it?"

The others peered at the spot where Tyler was pointing.

"It's very faint," said Wilf. "Do you think it means anything?"

Tyler pressed some keys on the Matrix. After a long time, the plasma globe lit up with a faint image.

"It's hard to say," said Tyler. "It looks like an island. The globe thinks it's in the West Indies, about 1792."

"It's worth checking out," said Wilma. "And I think Wilf and I should go. Our family came from the Caribbean."

“We’re all here on stand-by,” said Chip as Wilf and Wilma stepped into the portal. “Don’t forget to call us if you need us. You’ve got your Links and Zaptraps?”

“Yep! Will do!” grinned Wilf. He gave a salute as Tyler pressed the ‘send’ key. Then he and Wilma disappeared.

Being sucked back in time was not always an easy experience. As he slipped through time, Wilf heard voices chanting unfamiliar names. It gave him a strange feeling of dread in the pit of his stomach.

Chapter 4

Once they stepped out of the portal, the heat hit them. It was a sticky heat, filled with a moist, sweet, sickly smell.

"It's like the smell of grass being cut, only much sweeter," said Wilf.

Wilma was wearing a loose-fitting dress made of scratchy, coarse material. Wilf had canvas trousers and a rough shirt. They had no shoes on their feet.

They were at the top of a low hill. Behind them was the sea. Out in the bay were two ships under full sail. A beach fringed with palm trees stretched below them. But in front of them was an astonishing sight.

Fields of tall, leafy-stemmed plants grew as far as the eye could see.

"It's a sugar plantation," said Wilma. "Look, the sugar cane is being cut."

A line of about thirty men were cutting the thick canes. They moved together, first cutting the stems low down, then turning to throw the canes behind them.

Two or three at a time, the canes were dragged away by women and older children, and piled up. Other women and old men then stripped the leaves off the canes and loaded them into carts.

"The canes go to a mill to be crushed," said Wilma. "They collect the juice and boil it in huge cauldrons. That's what we can smell. It crystalizes into sugar. I read about it at school, on the internet."

One of the carts suddenly lurched and tipped over. The canes spilled out. The children pulling the cart flinched as a man ran up shouting at them.

The man, an overseer, struck the back of the biggest boy with a whip. "Take more care," he shouted.

"Oh no! That's cruel!" gasped Wilf. "This mission won't be easy. We don't even know what we're supposed to do!"

Wilma took out her Link and called Tyler. His crackly voice came back: "This one beats me. I can't work out what interest the Virans have in a sugar plantation."

Suddenly an ear-splitting sound like an explosion filled the air, followed by others. Boom ... boom ... boom!

Splashes could be heard, then splintering wood and shouting men.

"It's a sea battle," cried Wilma. "The bigger ship has caught the smaller one and it's attacking it."

At the sound of the battle, the slaves and overseers dropped what they were doing and raced over. Wilf and Wilma, who had hidden behind a bush, saw a chance to slip across and mingle with the plantation slaves.

Wilf heard one of the overseers say: "It's a British warship engaging a pirate ship."

The battle was soon over. Flames rose from the pirate ship. Then a huge explosion ripped its side out and at once it began to

sink. Some pirates launched a boat and scrambled in. Others dived into the sea.

An overseer cracked his whip. Another shouted at the slaves, “Right! The show’s over. Now get back to work, double quick.”

Wilf and Wilma hurried down the hill with a group of children. One of them asked, “Who are you? You don’ live here on this plantation. We h’ent seen you before.”

"Will you help us?" replied Wilma. "See, we're runaways from a plantation on the other side of the island. Been living rough."

"Beat ya too much, did they?" said a tall girl. "Course we'll help ya. Jus' work with us but mind Mr Rogers don' notice ya."

Wilf and Wilma helped pull the freshly cut sugar canes away and piled them up. It was hot work and Wilma felt the sweat running down her face.

"Don' slow down," urged the tall girl. "You don' want to get a beatin' in this plantation as well, do ya?"

Then, to Wilma's relief, there was another interruption. Two rough-looking men raced down the hill towards the plantation. Chasing them was a young midshipman, and two naval marines carrying muskets.

"Stop! In the name of the King," shouted the young officer. "Stop, or we'll fire!"

The men put their hands in the air and dropped to their knees before being seized by the marines.

The young officer called out to the overseers, "We act in the name of His Majesty, King George the Third. Our ship is HMS Nutmeg. These men are pirates. They plunder British vessels. They will be taken to Kingston to be tried.

One more man has escaped. If he comes here, do not shelter him. You are to arrest him."

The overseers cracked their whips again. "Excitement's over," one shouted. "Get back to work and make up for lost time."

At last, the day's toil was over. The slaves went to the huts where they lived. The tall girl, Melody, told everyone that Wilf and Wilma were runaways who needed food and shelter.

Wilma was tired and hungry, but she felt dreadful when she and Wilf were offered a wooden dish of rice with salt fish to eat.

"It's hard for them to spare us food," she whispered to Wilf. "Eat it and be grateful."

Then a loud moan, and a woman's cries of pain could be heard. Wilf looked startled.

"It's Mother," said Melody. "She's havin' a real hard time. Her baby has started, but baby ain't in no hurry to come."

Chapter 5

A woman stepped out of the darkness and into the firelight. She was carrying a bag and a bundle of clean white rags.

She spoke softly. "The overseers have sent for me. My name is Mercy Smith. I'm from the Williams Plantation. I was sent for because I have delivered many babies. I think, perhaps, you need my help."

"Am I glad you've come!" said Melody's father. "This baby is puttin' up a fight."

Wilma's Link buzzed. She slipped into the darkness and flipped it open. It was Tyler. "I'm on to something but I don't like it. Before he was killed, my father was a midshipman on a frigate called HMS Nutmeg. He was in action in the West Indies around 1792."

Wilma gasped. "This is so weird! HMS Nutmeg is in the bay. A midshipman came here earlier. It can't be your father, surely?"

Tyler gulped. "I need to ask Mortlock something," he said. "I'll get back to you."

Suddenly, a hand grabbed Wilma's arm. Someone had crept up on her out of the darkness. A stab of fear ran through her. Her hand went to her pocket for her Zaptrap, but both arms were pinned to her side and a hand was clamped over her mouth.

“Hush!” a voice said. “Don’t make a sound. I’m the runaway slave who escaped plantation life and became a pirate. Go and tell ’em Caleb Capstick needs help. Do it quietly. Don’t get ’em excited. I’m a hunted man. The overseers would love to get me, and so would the British Navy.”

With her heart thumping, Wilma hurried back and told Melody’s father. He and two other men went to where Wilma had encountered the pirate.

They had to carry Caleb back. He had been shot in the leg and had lost blood.

The slaves were excited. They had heard of Caleb Capstick, the slave who escaped and became a famous pirate. But Caleb told them, “You are in danger. If the overseers find out you have helped me it will be bad for all of you. All I need is a bandage for my bleeding leg and some food. I’ll rest for a while and be gone before daybreak.”

Mercy Smith came to see what all the excitement was about. "The baby won't be long," she said. "Its poor mother is worn out with so much pushing."

"Then you can help Caleb now by fixin' his leg," said Melody's father.

But the woman replied, "I got more important work to do. Fix it yourself."

"What's going on?" Wilf whispered to Wilma. "We don't seem to be picking up any clues. Nobody we've seen so far looks a bit like a Viran."

"I don't know either," replied Wilma. "Tyler thought he was on to something. It was to do with that ship that attacked the pirates, but he shut down the Link."

But then, Melody's father stood up.

"It is time to remember our roots. Our story must never be forgotten, even if it is a long time ago. You children must tell it with pride."

The slave children stood up. Melody began, "Once, our grandparents were free. They lived in Africa but ruthless men captured them to sell them as slaves."

A boy took up the story, speaking clearly, his eyes shining in the firelight.

He told how the slaves were transported across the Atlantic, chained together below decks in cramped and filthy conditions, and how so many died on that terrible voyage.

One by one the children chanted names – Abimola, Alaba, Dada, Eriole, Olufemi ...

Wilma found it unbearably sad. They were the names of slaves who had died on the voyage. She looked at Wilf and saw that he had tears running down his cheeks.

And at that instant, Wilma knew what the Virans' terrible plan was.

Chapter 6

Then, confusion! A voice roared, "Nobody move!" The young naval officer and his marines burst in with the overseers. "Where is Capstick?" he shouted. "We know you're hiding him."

Wilma whispered urgently to Wilf. "The Virans are going to wipe Tyler out. This is what it's all about."

"Wipe him out? I don't understand," said Wilf. "What's Tyler got to do with it?"

"Tyler comes from the past, right? He thinks this midshipman will one day be his father. So if this officer is just a youngster now, new to the sea and not married, what if he is killed?"

"If he's killed, Tyler could never have existed ... oh my ... !" gasped Wilf.

Then Capstick leapt forward. There was a blur of movement and the flash of a knife, as the pirate seized the midshipman and spun him round. Before anyone could move, the pirate had the knife pressed to the midshipman's throat.

"He's the Viran!" cried Wilma.

She hurled her Zaptrap at Capstick. It flew into the darkness but did not open.

"Don't try anything," Capstick shouted.

"It's been nice meeting you but I must decline the hospitality of King George."

He backed away using the midshipman as a shield and melted into the darkness. One marine raised his musket to his shoulder.

"No!" gasped Wilma. Thinking the man might be the Viran, Wilf threw his Zaptrap. It sailed into the night but did not activate.

Then the midshipman came back. “Are you all right, Mr Collins?” asked one of the soldiers.

“I’m fine, but Capstick’s gone, curse him. He let me go. Ran off into the sugar cane.”

Wilf and Wilma had the same thought. “Tyler’s name is Watts,” said Wilma. “But that man’s name is Collins. So now what do we do?”

Chapter 7

The strange woman had walked in out of the night. She had come to help with the birth of a child and everyone had believed her story.

The truth hit Wilma like a thunderbolt.

"Mercy Smith!" she cried. "She's the Viran. Don't you see, Wilf? It's you and me that the Virans mean to wipe out!"

“What if Melody’s parents are our ancestors? Then the baby is our great-great-great-great-grandparent! If the baby doesn’t survive it will be us who won’t exist! If Mercy is the Viran, we’ve got to do something.”

“But we’ve lost our Zaptraps. What can we do?” said Wilf, in panic.

“I don’t know. But we can’t do *nothing*! Come on!”

Wilma ran into the hut as the tiny cry of a baby could be heard. An old woman was helping Mercy. Wilma asked to see the baby.

Mercy had it wrapped in a white cloth. She turned away, speaking softly, “Ah! There is something wrong. I must …”

Wilma rushed at Mercy Smith, crashing into her and sending her off balance.

“Grab the baby, Wilf!” Wilma yelled.

In surprise, Mercy let the baby go. She gave a hiss of anger. Her face changed into one of Viran fury. Her eyes became reptile eyes, her hand a claw that grabbed something from her apron and threw it.

The smothersphere burst open. Swirls of blackness like tentacles wound round Wilma and curled towards Wilf. There was a scream.

A sound like an angry insect flew towards the Viran. A Zaptrap! In an instant, the Viran became a huge, cold flame of crackling energy and was gone. The Zaptrap snapped shut and fell to the ground. The inky blackness evaporated.

"Flippin' 'eck," said Tyler. "I've never seen a Zaptrap work for real. Looks like I arrived in the nick of time."

Tyler was standing there with a pair of crutches. "Mortlock wouldn't let me come," he explained. "But I had to see my father."

Wilf looked at the baby gurgling happily in his arms. "Meet my great-great-great-great grandfather. This is who the Viran was after, not your dad."

He handed the baby to the old woman.

Melody and her father, along with others, crowded into the hut to see the baby.

Outside, Wilma saw the midshipman about to leave. "Excuse me," she called. "Is there an officer on your ship called Midshipman Watts?"

The officer gave Wilf, Wilma and Tyler a suspicious look. But he told them that the previous year, Midshipman Watts had been transferred to another ship, called HMS Firefly.

"We'd better get back to the Time Vault," said Wilma. "Report to Mortlock. See what he thinks of this latest move by the Virans."

"Yeah, Mortlock! He told me I wasn't to come, but I ignored him."

"So how did you 'send' yourself," asked Wilf, "once you were in the portal?"

Tyler gave a grin. "Let's get back, and I'll show you!"

Glossary

frigate *(page 27)* A battleship built for speed, the frigate's main task was patrolling the high seas. *"... my father was a midshipman on a frigate called HMS Nutmeg."*

midshipman *(page 23)* A seaman whose authority is greater than the ordinary sailors, but who has the lowest rank of any officer. They are therefore between (or 'mid') a sailor and an officer. *Chasing them was a young midshipman, and two naval marines carrying muskets.*

muskets *(page 23)* An old-fashioned long-barrelled rifle. It was not very accurate.

naval marines *(page 23)* A soldier belonging to the Navy, trained to fight both at sea and on land.

plantation *(page 16)* A farm or large area of land, planted with crops such as sugarcane, coffee, tea or rubber. *"It's a sugar plantation," said Wilma.*

thwarted *(page 3)* When someone's plans are prevented from happening. *"We have been thwarted in our purpose because of children."*

Thesaurus: Another word for ...

thwarted (*page 3*) foiled, hindered, prevented, impeded.

Tyler's Mission Report

Location:	Date:
St. Ann's Bay, Jamaica.	1792
Mission Status:	**Viran Status:**
Successful / Case closed.	1 zaptrapped.

Notes: It's history, but this time it's personal!

So many mixed feelings ... To see my father again ... I'd never thought of using the TimeWeb to find him. But then, what would I have said to him? Could I have told him that I knew he was going to be killed at sea? And how could he explain what he was doing out there? To discover your father was part of the slave trade, even if not directly part of it... Did he ever wonder if what his country was doing was wrong? But then, even if he did, what could he have done about it? I have no answers. But I do know that every person has rights. The very human rights that my mother's country, France, was establishing in those same years. The slave trade was a dark moment in history. And yet it is still part of Wilf and Wilma's history. Part of their family story.

Sign off: Tyler

History: downloaded!

The Slave Trade

Slave trading began about 1630. Ships would carry goods to West Africa. Some goods would be sold but most would be exchanged for enslaved Africans who were then taken in the same ships to America and the Caribbean. These ships would then return to Europe carrying rum, sugar, tobacco, rice and cotton. It was a very profitable and it made the merchants and ship-owners very rich.

William Wilberforce helped to end the slave trade in Britain

The passage across the Atlantic was terrible for the slaves. They were packed into tight spaces below decks and given barely enough food and water to stay alive. Hundreds of them died while being transported.

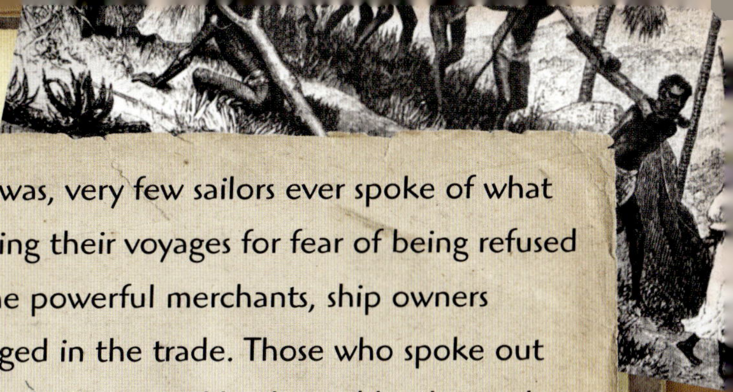

Sugar cane

Terrible though it was, very few sailors ever spoke of what they had seen during their voyages for fear of being refused further work by the powerful merchants, ship owners and captains engaged in the trade. Those who spoke out against the slave trade were quickly silenced by those who stood to lose money if slavery was abolished.

The slave trade was abolished in 1807, but it was not until 1833 that Britain passed the Abolition of Slavery Act.

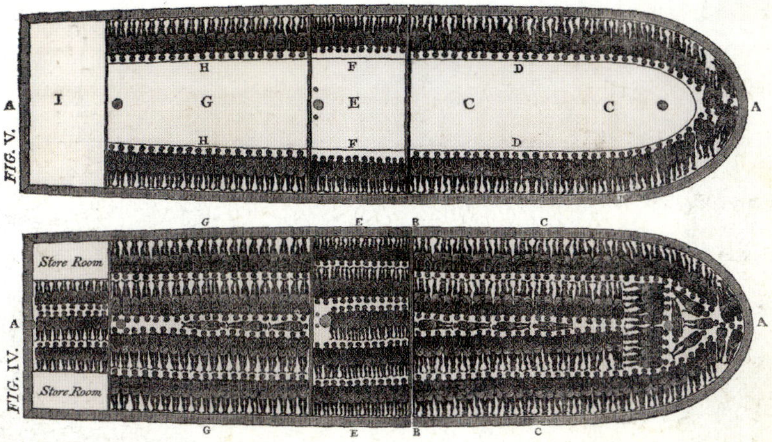

This plan shows how overcrowded a slave ship could be and yet still remain within the legally permitted capacity.

For more information, see the Time Chronicles website:
www.oxfordprimary.co.uk/timechronicles

A voice from history

I was born into slavery. Many of us died young because of poor food, cruelty and hard labour. We have no rights, not even the most basic freedoms. Not even the right to protect our own families.

Many workers on this plantation are girls like me, and women. I began work at four years old, collecting grass to feed the mules and oxen. By ten I was weeding the cane fields, and helping with the harvest. By eighteen I will be toiling in the fields planting the sugar canes. By 40, if I live that long, I'll be worn out, and I expect I'll be sent back to feeding the livestock. If I survive a few more years, I might become a nurse to the babies on the plantation. And what will their lives be like? The same as mine – working to make the plantation owners and sugar merchants rich.